Editor
Eric Migliaccio

Contributing Editor
Wanda Kelly

Managing Editor
Ina Massler Levin, M.A.

Editor-in-Chief
Sharon Coan, M.S. Ed.

Cover Artist
Barb Lorseyedi

Art Coordinator
Kevin Barnes

Imaging
James Edward Grace

Product Manager
Phil Garcia

Publisher
Mary D. Smith, M.S. Ed.

Grammar, Usage & Mechanics

GRADE 4

Author

Wanda Kelly

Teacher Created Resources, Inc.
6421 Industry Way
Westminster, CA 92683
www.teachercreated.com
ISBN-0-7439-3347-8
©*2002 Teacher Created Resources, Inc.*
Reprinted, 2005
Made in U.S.A.

W9-DID-993

Table of Contents

Introduction

The old adage "practice makes perfect" can really hold true for your child and his or her education. The more your child has practice with and exposure to concepts being taught in school, the more success he or she is likely to achieve. For many parents, knowing how to help their children may be frustrating because the resources may not be readily available.

As a parent, it is also difficult to know where to focus your efforts so that the extra practice your child receives at home supports what he or she is learning in school.

This book has been written to help parents and teachers reinforce basic skills with children. *Practice Makes Perfect: Grammar, Usage, and Mechanics* reviews basic grammar skills for fourth graders. The exercises in this book can be done sequentially or can be taken out of order, as needed.

The following standards or objectives will be met or reinforced by completing the practice pages included in this book. These standards and objectives are similar to the ones required by your state and school district because they are considered appropriate for fourth graders:

- The student can identify and use declarative, imperative, interrogative, and exclamatory sentences.
- The student can identify and use various forms of nouns and pronouns: common and proper nouns and singular and plural nouns and pronouns.
- The student can identify and use various forms of verbs: past tense, present tense, action.
- The student can identify and use adjectives and adverbs.
- The student uses coordinating conjunctions to link ideas.
- The student uses negative forms correctly.
- The student can spell correctly words commonly used at the fourth-grade level.
- The student follows the conventions of capitalization: titles; proper nouns; first words of direct quotations; and words used in the heading, salutation, and closing of a letter.
- The student follows the conventions of punctuation: periods, commas, apostrophes, and quotation marks.

How to Make the Most of This Book

Here are some useful ideas for making the most of this book:

- Set aside a specific place in your home to work on this book. Keep it neat and tidy, with the necessary materials on hand.
- Set up a certain time of day to work on these practice pages to establish consistency; or look for times in your day or week that are less hectic and more conducive to practicing skills.
- Keep all practice sessions with your child positive and constructive. If your child becomes frustrated or tense, set the book aside and look for another time to practice. Forcing your child to perform will not help. Do not use this book as a punishment.
- Help your beginning reader with instructions.
- Review the work your child has done.
- Allow your child to use whatever writing instruments he or she prefers. For example, using colored pencils can add variety and pleasure to drill work.
- Pay attention to the areas in which your child has the most difficulty. Provide extra guidance and exercises in those areas.

Identifying Sentences

☞ Declarative sentences make statements: *I like ice cream.*

☞ Imperative sentences make requests or give commands: *Buy me some ice cream.*

☞ Interrogative sentences ask questions: *Should I get one scoop or two?*

☞ Exclamatory sentences (which are often short sentences) express strong feeling: *This ice cream is fantastic!*

(*Helpful Hint:* End punctuation for declarative and imperative sentences is the period. Interrogative sentences end with question marks, and exclamatory sentences end with exclamation points.)

Label the following sentences **D** (declarative), **IP** (imperative), **IT** (interrogative), or **E** (exclamatory).

1. _____ Yesterday Rosa, Lucille, Ricardo, and Luke went to the Uptown Mall to shop for clothes.

2. _____ Do you think this olive green shirt looks good on me?

3. _____ Let's buy it right now!

4. _____ Go to the salesperson and tell her you want to buy it.

5. _____ Where is she?

6. _____ I don't see anyone around here who is a salesperson.

7. _____ Perhaps they are all at lunch and there is no one here to sell things to us.

8. _____ That is impossible!

9. _____ Oh, look at this!

10. _____ This is the most beautiful jacket I have ever seen, Rosa.

11. _____ Lucille, I think you should buy it.

12. _____ But I don't want to buy a jacket unless Ricardo is also going to get one.

13. _____ That's silly!

14. _____ Okay, I will buy the jacket.

15. _____ Where did that salesperson go?

Composing Sentences

1. Write four *declarative* sentences about a friend or pet.

   a. _____

   b. _____

   c. _____

   d. _____

2. Write four *imperative* sentences as if you were writing them to a friend or sibling.

   a. _____

   b. _____

   c. _____

   d. _____

3. Write four *interrogative* sentences as if you were writing them to a parent or teacher.

   a. _____

   b. _____

   c. _____

   d. _____

4. Write four *exclamatory* sentences as if you were writing about some kind of contest (a race, for example).

   a. _____

   b. _____

   c. _____

   d. _____

Assessment: Types of Sentences

Write responses to the following sentences by using the kinds of sentences listed.

1. I think that I have never seen a more beautiful sunset. **(interrogative)**

   _____

2. Someone has been in your room and rearranged your belongings. **(exclamatory)**

   _____

3. You want your friend to go with you to talk to the teacher. **(imperative)**

   _____

4. Do you think your grades will be above average by the end of the year? **(declarative)**

   _____

5. Your pet has disappeared.

   (interrogative sentence) _____

   (imperative sentence) _____

   (declarative sentence) _____

   (exclamatory sentence) _____

6. You have just learned that you have been selected to be on the next spaceship to Mars.

   (interrogative sentence) _____

   (imperative sentence) _____

   (declarative sentence) _____

   (exclamatory sentence) _____

Identifying Common and Proper Nouns

A noun is a word that names something.

☞ Common nouns name general people, places, or things.

☞ Proper nouns name specific people, places, or things.

Use the lines before them to label the following nouns **C** for common nouns or **P** for proper nouns. On the lines after the nouns, write a matching proper noun after each common noun and a matching common noun after each proper noun.

Examples: 1. __P__ Asia _____continent_____

2. __C__ continent _____Antarctica_____

1. _____ England _____

2. _____ day _____

3. _____ month _____

4. _____ Monday _____

5. _____ April _____

6. _____ Venus _____

7. _____ Chicago _____

8. _____ France _____

9. _____ Mother's Day _____

10. _____ ocean _____

11. _____ mountain _____

12. _____ country _____

13. _____ Iowa _____

14. _____ Mt. McKinley _____

15. _____ Lake Ontario _____

16. _____ holiday _____

17. _____ city _____

18. _____ island _____

19. _____ dog _____

20. _____ elephant _____

21. _____ Chevrolet _____

22. _____ teacher _____

23. _____ president _____

24. _____ mayor _____

25. _____ planet _____

26. _____ school _____

27. _____ Mrs. Brown _____

28. _____ Granny Smith _____

29. _____ song _____

30. _____ poem _____

Creating and Using Plural Noun Forms

Nouns can be identified as singular or plural. Their plurals are formed in various ways:

◆ by adding *s* (example: cat—cats),

◆ by adding *es* (example: box—boxes),

◆ by changing a *y* to *i* and adding *es* (example: puppy—puppies),

◆ by changing *f* or *fe* to *v* and adding *es* (example: knife—knives), and

◆ by changing a vowel inside the word (example: man—men).

(Helpful Hint: Some nouns—like *sheep*—have the same form for both singular and plural.)

Write the plural forms of the following nouns and then use the plural form of each in a sentence.

1. pony ___ponies___

___

2. chief ___chieves___

___

3. dance ___dances___

___

4. zebra ___zebras___

___

5. radio ___radios___

___

6. orange ___oranges___

___

7. dress ___dresses___

___

8. bush ___bushes___

___

9. piano ___pianos___

___

10. rodeo ___rodeos___

___

Creating and Using Plural Noun Forms *(cont.)*

11. hero _____

_____

12. country _____

_____

13. enemy _____

_____

14. fish _____

_____

15. thief _____

_____

16. mouse _____

_____

17. woman _____

_____

18. deer _____

_____

19. toothbrush _____

_____

20. Jane _____

_____

21. Barnes _____

_____

22. Mary _____

_____

Identifying and Using Pronouns

Pronouns are words that are used in place of nouns. Like nouns, personal pronouns are used as both subjects and objects in sentences.

Rewrite the sentences below using personal pronouns (*I, you, he, she, it, we, they, me, him, her, us, them*) to replace the nouns in bold print.

1. **Luke** played baseball. _____

2. Mom read **the new bestseller**. _____

3. **Lucille** swam across the pool. _____

4. **The girls** walked to Mary's house. _____

5. **Lucille and Luke** climbed trees. _____

6. The team gave **Lucille** a trophy. _____

7. Rosa saw **the dog** run away. _____

8. **My dad** put gas in the car. _____

9. Ricardo saw **the strange man**. _____

10. Where is **the key**? _____

11. **The key** is here! _____

12. Where should I put **the presents**? _____

13. **Rosa** put the presents away. _____

14. Ricardo, give this to **Rosa**. _____

15. **Lucille** is coming to my house. _____

16. I gave **Luke** the book to read. _____

17. **Rosa and I** are wearing dresses. _____

18. Are **Rosa and Luke** at home? _____

19. **The book** is on the table. _____

20. **Ricardo and his friends** arrived. _____

Identifying and Using Pronouns *(cont.)*

Use each of the personal pronouns listed below in a sentence.

1. it _____

   _____

2. us _____

   _____

3. he _____

   _____

4. she _____

   _____

5. you _____

   _____

6. me _____

   _____

7. I _____

   _____

8. we _____

   _____

9. they _____

   _____

10. them _____

    _____

11. her _____

    _____

12. him _____

    _____

Identifying and Using Verbs

Add an action verb (example: *call*, *run*, *write*) to complete each sentence.

1. Rosa _____caught_____ the ball I threw her.

2. Lucille _____pushed_____ the button on the computer.

3. Ricardo's horse _____ran_____ across the pasture.

4. Luke's watchdog _____bit_____ the burglar's leg.

5. The students may _____leave_____ when the bell rings.

6. Rosa and Lucille _____ three miles every day.

7. "_____!" yelled Lucille to Ricardo.

8. The teacher _____ the class about chewing gum.

9. They _____ clear across town.

10. Luke _____ a letter to his friend in New York.

Write a sentence using each past tense verb.

11. shouted _____

12. drove _____

13. became _____

14. dived _____

15. drowned _____

16. rose _____

17. went _____

18. swam _____

19. set _____

20. stole _____

Identifying and Using Verbs *(cont.)*

The following sentences are written in the present tense. Rewrite them in the past tense.

Examples: *present tense*—I am a skater.

past tense—I was a skater.

1. Ricardo and Lucille play soccer. _____

_____

2. Rosa and Luke are the best soccer players. _____

_____

3. Their teacher is absent. _____

_____

4. I break some fragile object every day. _____

_____

5. Jack and Jill climb the hill to fetch water. _____

_____

6. Ricardo draws gruesome pictures of monsters. _____

_____

7. I understand what you said. _____

_____

8. Lucille writes in her journal every evening. _____

_____

9. Rosa loses her money often. _____

_____

10. Ricardo trips over his own feet. _____

_____

Identifying and Using Verbs *(cont.)*

Complete each sentence by writing the past tense of the verb in parentheses.

1. Luke _____ the school bell. (**ring**)

2. Ricardo _____ his bicycle. (**ride**)

3. Lucille _____ ghosts. (**see**)

4. Rosa _____ the candy. (**eat**)

5. Lucy and Rosa _____ home. (**run**)

Rewrite each of the above sentences with the verb in the future tense.

6. _____

7. _____

8. _____

9. _____

10. _____

Underline all the verbs (present, past, and future tenses) in the following paragraph.

This is the year I plan improvements in my grades in school. Last year I had only average grades. My parents said they thought my grades were acceptable. I was glad they felt that way. However, I think that hard work raises a student's grades. Everyone tells me this is true, and I believe them. I now plan my days around school and homework. All other activities come after that. It seems to me that is the first step toward improvement. I know that if I succeed in school, the rewards will come. One reward will be more knowledge. Another reward will be good work habits. A further reward will be a chance for a better future.

Identifying and Using Adjectives

Adjectives are used to perform the following functions in sentences:

◆ to describe nouns and pronouns,

◆ to limit or show the number of things or the numerical order of things,

◆ to point out which noun is being referred to, and

◆ to make comparisons.

Complete each sentence by adding the correct adjective from the box.

soft	**strong**	**empty**	**raw**	**fast**	**open**

1. Rosa put some hot water in the _____ bucket.

2. Luke and Ricardo went through the _____ door.

3. Lucille's cheetah is a very _____ runner.

4. Rosa's feather pillow is especially _____ .

5. The _____ meat was placed in the skillet by Luke.

6. Ricardo's elephant is a very _____ animal.

Complete each sentence by adding the correct adjective from the box.

brown	**red**	**white**	**black**	**green**	**blue**

7. Penelope, Rosa's pet cow, ate the _____ grass.

8. The piece of coal that Luke picked up was _____ .

9. Ricardo dived into the _____ water of the Black Sea.

10. Lucille decided to eat the _____ strawberry.

11. Luke's milk was not brown chocolate milk but instead was _____ .

12. However, the chocolate bar that Rosa ate was _____ .

Identifying and Using Adjectives (cont.)

Complete each sentence by adding the correct adjective from the box.

| five | eight | twelve | four | two | seven |

1. There are _____ months in the year.
2. You have _____ fingers on each hand.
3. An octopus has _____ tentacles.
4. There are _____ days in the week.
5. Most bicycles have _____ wheels.
6. Most cars have _____ wheels.

Complete each sentence by adding a correct adjective from the box.

| this | that | these | those |

7. _____ gloves are mine, but _____ gloves are Rosa's.
8. _____ glass belongs to me, and _____ glass is yours, Luke.
9. _____ books are mine, and _____ books are yours, Lucille.
10. _____ boxes were removed, but _____ boxes were left.

Complete each sentence by adding a correct adjective from the box.

| my | their | her | its | our | your |

11. Ricardo's cat licked _____ paws.
12. _____ best friend is exceedingly amusing.
13. Is that _____ car in the garage, Rosa?
14. _____ dress and earrings were very expensive.
15. It was _____ dog that bit _____ dog.

Identifying and Using Adjectives *(cont.)*

Fill in the blanks to show the positive, comparative, and superlative degrees for the following adjectives. An example has been done for you.

	Positive Degree	Comparative Degree	Superlative Degree
1.	smooth	smoother	smoothest
2.			thinnest
3.		luckier	
4.	wise		
5.		more delicate	
6.			greenest
7.	good	better	
8.			most beautiful

Complete each sentence by using the comparative or superlative degree of the adjective in parentheses.

9. Luke is _____ than Ricardo. (**strong**)

10. Ricardo is the _____ boy in the school. (**reliable**)

11. This table is _____ than that one. (**heavy**)

12. This pie is _____ than that one. (**delicious**)

13. Ms. Lee is the _____ person I know. (**brave**)

14. This is the _____ day we have had all year. (**hot**)

15. This Gala apple is _____ than the one you are eating. (**red**)

16. This is the _____ place of all to hide. (**safe**)

17. Today is _____ than yesterday was. (**cold**)

18. Rosa is the _____ person in the fourth grade. (**noisy**)

19. Lucille thinks she is _____ than you are. (**lucky**)

20. A Clydesdale is one of the _____ horses there is. (**big**)

Identifying and Using Adverbs

Adverbs are used to perform the following functions in sentences:

◆ to add meaning to a verb, an adjective, or another adverb;

◆ to show how, when, or where something happened; and

◆ to show degrees of comparison.

Complete each sentence by choosing an adverb from the box.

noisily	easily	slowly	greedily	silently	gently

1. Lucille's very hungry dog _____ ate the meat.

2. Mrs. Lucky _____ put her baby to bed.

3. Luke's cat Capricorn _____ crept after the mouse.

4. Rosa, the fastest runner, _____ won the race.

5. Ricardo _____ walked down the street on a broken leg.

6. When our teacher left the room, we began to work _____.

Compose sentences that use the listed adverbs.

7. softly _____

8. quickly _____

9. carefully _____

10. sadly _____

Change the word in parentheses into an adverb to complete each sentence.

11. Lucy _____ swam across the English Channel. (**strong**)

12. Ricky _____ eyed the remaining cookie in the jar. (**sad**)

13. Luke always does his schoolwork very _____. (**neat**)

14. Rosa watched as the train came _____ into the station. (**slow**)

15. Our teacher always checks our homework very _____. (**careful**)

Identifying and Using Adverbs *(cont.)*

Complete each sentence by choosing an adverb from the box.

out	**here**	**there**	**near**

1. The supermarket Lucille goes to is not far; in fact, it is quite _____.

2. Our teacher told us to put the extra book _____.

3. The terrible car accident Ricardo was in occurred right _____.

4. Luke came in the back door as we went _____.

Complete each sentence by choosing an adverb from the box. (Hints are provided in the parentheses.)

often	**now**	**yesterday**	**soon**

5. Ricardo has missed his piano lesson _____. **(many times)**

6. We are sure Lucy will arrive _____. **(in a short time)**

7. Do not wait for a moment; write your paragraph _____. **(right away)**

8. Ricardo and Luke went swimming _____. **(the day before today)**

Fill in the blanks to show the positive, comparative, and superlative degrees for the following adverbs.

	Positive Degree	Comparative Degree	Superlative Degree
9.	hard		
10.		more softly	
11.			best
12.	easy		
13.		faster	

Using Coordinating Conjunctions

Conjunctions can join compound subjects and compound predicates as well as serve to create compound sentences. The three most commonly used coordinating conjunctions are *and*, *but*, and *or*.

Make each pair of sentences into one sentence by using *and*, *but*, or *or* to create compound subjects, compound predicates, or compound sentences. Remember to put a comma before the conjunction when you join two complete sentences.

1. Jacqueline has a cat. Jacqueline has a dog. _____

   _____

2. Would you like vanilla ice cream? Would you rather have chocolate? _____

   _____

3. I was going to play. I decided to do homework. _____

   _____

4. Mother told me to come inside. I stayed outside. _____

   _____

5. After school I have a swimming lesson. After school I have a piano lesson. _____

   _____

6. One of my favorite colors is blue. Another favorite color is yellow. _____

   _____

7. I was going to ride my bike. It had a flat tire. _____

   _____

8. We can have pizza for lunch. We can have a hot dog for lunch. _____

   _____

Using Coordinating Conjunctions *(cont.)*

Combine the following pairs of sentences with *or, and,* or *but.* Remember to place a comma before the coordinating conjunction when combining two complete sentences.

1. You can wear your blue jeans. You can wear your black jeans. _____

   _____

2. Your white T-shirt fits better. Your red T-shirt is more colorful. _____

   _____

3. Do you want yellow patches on your jeans? Do you want pink patches on your jeans?

   _____

   _____

4. Jillian's T-shirt looks attractive. Jacqueline's jeans are stunning. _____

   _____

5. I have three pairs of blue jeans. I want another pair of blue jeans. _____

   _____

6. You can wash your old jeans. You can iron your new jeans. _____

   _____

7. This white T-shirt is mine. That white T-shirt is yours. _____

   _____

8. Let's wear our blue jeans today. Let's wear our red jeans tomorrow. _____

   _____

9. My old jeans fit me well. My new jeans do not fit me very well. _____

   _____

10. I have washed my new red T-shirt. I have not washed my new blue T-shirt. _____

   _____

Identifying and Using Negative Forms

Only one negative word is used to make a negative statement.

Examples: *correct*—Lucy has barely paid for her dress.

incorrect—Lucy hasn't barely paid for her dress.

Indicate with a **C** those sentences that correctly express negative statements. Use an **I** for those sentences that are incorrect.

1. _____ Nobody can't say that Ricardo doesn't work as hard as he can.

2. _____ Lucille could hardly hear what Rosa was saying to the boys.

3. _____ There is but one fourth grade student on the decorating committee.

4. _____ Rosa couldn't hardly hear what Lucille was saying to her.

5. _____ "I haven't no money," said Luke.

6. _____ No one ever gave the book to Ricky.

7. _____ Lucy's mother told her that she hasn't but one dollar.

8. _____ There isn't but one orange left in the bowl on the counter.

9. _____ Rosa's daily complaint is that she hasn't no money.

10. _____ It is true that Ricardo has not never paid his own way to the movies.

Use the listed words to write sentences that correctly express negative statements.

11. never _____

12. no _____

13. nobody _____

14. none _____

15. nothing _____

16. no one _____

17. hardly _____

18. scarcely _____

Identifying and Using Articles

The words *a, an,* and *the* are called articles in grammar and function in sentences as adjectives because they limit or modify nouns and pronouns, just as other adjectives do.

☞ The definite article *the* is used to indicate a specific noun or pronoun.

☞ The articles *a* and *an* are used when no particular noun or pronoun is being pointed out. *An* is used when the word it precedes begins with a vowel sound.

(*Helpful Hint:* The articles can be used to determine whether or not a word is a noun. If a word makes sense or can be used in a sentence with an article before it, that word can function as a noun.)

Use *a, an,* or *the* in the spaces in the sentences and then in the paragraph.

1. Lucy can only do _____ underarm throw.

2. She would like to be _____ professional athlete when she grows up.

3. Ricardo thinks that _____ miracle will have to occur before that happens.

4. According to Rosa _____ elf lives in her grandmother's garden.

5. Do you think that is _____ truth?

6. Luke says that _____ elf is about one foot tall and has red hair.

7. Lucille is still _____ fastest runner in our school.

8. Perhaps she will become _____ professional runner.

9. However, Ricardo thinks that such _____ thing is not likely to happen.

10. She might have _____ better chance of becoming a physical fitness trainer.

The Bad Sport

There is (11.) _____ boy in my class who is (12.) _____ best football player in (13.) _____ school. He is (14.) _____ very good swimmer, too, but he is not (15.) _____ good citizen because he has (16.) _____ bad temper. One day he threw (17.) _____ football through (18.) _____ open door. It hit (19.) _____ boy who was sitting in (20.) _____ old chair near (21.) _____ table that belongs to (22.) _____ teacher. (23.) _____ teacher was upset and told (24.) _____ boy that he would not be allowed to go on (25.) _____ field trip the whole class will be taking later this month.

Identifying and Using Prepositions and Prepositional Phrases

Prepositions and their objects usually are used to indicate the positions of things or people. The object of a preposition will be a noun or pronoun. (*Helpful Hint:* The object may have one or more adjectives before it.)

Example: Jacqueline's canary sleeps in a cage.

in—preposition

in a cage—prepositional phrase

a—adjective (modifying *cage*)

cage—noun (object of the preposition)

Complete each sentence by choosing a preposition from the box. Use each word only once. Then, underline the rest of the prepositional phrase.

on	**into**	**in**	**before**	**toward**
over	**under**	**inside**	**below**	**beside**

1. A shiny black crow is sitting _____ a nest.

2. The striped snake is crawling _____ its hole.

3. A tawny kitten was sleeping _____ the dining table.

4. In Australia you may see a kangaroo hopping _____ a fence.

5. Our family dog sleeps _____ his very own house.

6. The white horse ran into the barn _____ the black horse.

7. The baby porpoise was swimming _____ her mother.

8. At the zoo we saw the elephant swing his trunk _____ the fence.

9. The bald eagle was watching everything that was going on _____ his high perch.

10. Boswell, our terrier, does not like to go _____ our house.

Assessment: Parts of Speech

1. In this following paragraph . . .

   - underline once all the words used as nouns. (Remember to check for nouns by using one of the articles.)

   - put two lines under each personal pronoun.

   - circle each verb.

> My mother is an outstanding cook. She carefully prepared a delicious cake last year and easily won a prize at the local fair. After she expertly added flour and other ingredients to her bowl, she quickly cracked a fresh egg and dropped the yellow yolk and the sticky white into the red mixing bowl with the rest of the tasty ingredients. After she swiftly mixed everything, she put the batter in a pan and then into the hot oven for forty minutes. When it was ready, she put the prizewinning cake on a plate and cut it with a sharp knife. We all enjoyed that special cake.

2. In this following paragraph . . .

   - underline all the words used as adjectives (including articles and pronouns) with one line.

   - underline the adverbs with two lines.

   - circle all the prepositional phrases.

> My father is an outstanding fisherman. He skillfully caught a 10-pound rainbow trout last year and easily won a prize at the fishing tournament. First he carefully prepared his pole and line. Then he expertly tied a fly and attached it to the line. Dad next headed for his favorite spot on the river. It is a deep pool where the river curves. He found the perfect place and flicked his line into the water. After a half hour he felt a soft nibble. Then the fish struck. My dad knew he had a big fish. However, he expressed the greatest joy when he learned he had caught a 10-pound rainbow trout. After he officially weighed it and recorded it with the tournament committee, he brought it home. My mother cooked it, and our family ate the prizewinning trout.

Assessment: Parts of Speech (cont.)

Write sentences that contain the parts of speech listed in parentheses—and in the order listed. You may add other elements, too.

1. **(noun, verb)**

   _____

   _____

   _____

2. **(adjective, noun, verb)**

   _____

   _____

   _____

3. **(adjective, noun, verb, adverb)**

   _____

   _____

   _____

4. **(adjective, noun, adverb, verb, prepositional phrase)**

   _____

   _____

   _____

5. **(prepositional phrase, noun, verb, adverb)**

   _____

   _____

   _____

Identifying and Spelling Homophones

A homophone is a word that sounds the same as another word but has a different meaning and different spelling.

Use a word from the box to complete each sentence.

poor	**tail**	**pour**	**tale**
wood	**hear**	**would**	**here**

1. Our teacher told us a _____ about a dinosaur.

2. Did you _____ the roar of the lions at the zoo?

3. Ricardo and Luke cut some _____ to make a campfire.

4. I asked Lucille to _____ the water in the bottle.

5. Rosa's dog spun around and tried to bite its own _____.

6. I asked Ms. Lucky to leave the books right _____.

7. Luke was too _____ to buy even a hamburger for lunch.

8. Ricky said he _____ come if he had his parents' permission.

Underline the correct words in the parentheses.

9. Lucy told Rosa it is rude to (**stair, stare**) at people.

10. They watched the old ship being (**towed, toad**) out to sea to be sunk.

11. Did you (**meet, meat**) our new teacher, Ricardo?

12. Luke brushed his favorite horse's (**main, mane**).

13. Our family's new automobile is made of a special kind of (**steal, steel**).

14. Unfortunately, Lucille's mother was too (**weak, week**) to leave the hospital.

15. Our parents tell us we should not (**medal, meddle**) in other people's business.

16. Luke (**rode, road**) up on his favorite horse, Bronco.

17. It is almost time for our daily (**male, mail**) delivery.

18. I used stone-ground (**flower, flour**) to make the biscuits.

Identifying and Spelling Homographs

A homograph is a word that is spelled the same as another word but has a different meaning.

Use a word from the box to complete each sentence. Use each word twice.

bark	**rock**	**bank**

1. Chan's golden retriever began to _____.

2. Lucy discovered that the _____ of the Chattahoochee River was steep.

3. Ricardo saw the foolish boy throw a _____ at his neighbor's window.

4. I like to save all my money in my account at the _____.

5. We screamed as the huge waves began to _____ the sailboat.

6. Rosa made a canoe from the _____ of a tree for her social studies project.

Write two sentences for each word. Make sure that the meanings of the word in the two sentences are different.

post

7. _____

_____

8. _____

_____

well

9. _____

_____

10. _____

_____

bat

11. _____

12. _____

_____

Identifying Root Words

A root word is a word from which other words are built. Prefixes and suffixes are added to root words to alter their meanings.

Example: **root word**—appear
prefix added—dis-appear
suffix added—disappear-ance

Write the root words for the following words.

1. indoors _____
2. unwashed _____
3. disagreement _____
4. awaken _____
5. unfinished _____
6. enjoyable _____
7. unbolted _____
8. telephoned _____
9. untruthful _____
10. unclaimed _____

11. unreasonable _____
12. disrespectful _____
13. informally _____
14. imprisonment _____
15. uncertainty _____
16. unsuitable _____
17. unmistakable _____
18. dishonorable _____
19. unbreakable _____
20. reconstruction _____

First write five words of your own that have prefixes. Then write five words of your own that have suffixes.

Prefix
21. _____
22. _____
23. _____
24. _____
25. _____

Suffix
26. _____
27. _____
28. _____
29. _____
30. _____

Creating Compound Words

Compound words are words made by joining two or more words together.

Add a word from the box to complete each compound word in the sentence.

mother	**ache**	**brush**	**fish**	**quake**
where	**coat**	**prints**	**corn**	**pan**

1. At the beach Lucy and Rosa saw a jelly_____.

2. Luke cooked eggs in the sauce_____.

3. Ricardo likes to eat pop_____ for lunch.

4. Lucille's grand_____ rides a motorbike.

5. I cleaned my teeth with a tooth_____.

6. A terrible earth_____ struck San Francisco.

7. Luke's head_____ is very painful.

8. Because it was cold outside, Ricardo wore an over_____.

9. Rosa could see the foot_____ in the snow.

10. Lucille and Luke searched every_____ for the missing money.

The parts of these compound words have been mixed up. Write them correctly on the lines below. An example has been done for you.

strawlight	**moonball**	**photoboat**	**lifecuffs**
berryfoot	**graphnote**	**breakhand**	**fastbook**

11. _____strawberry_____   15. _____

12. _____   16. _____

13. _____   17. _____

14. _____   18. _____

Assessment: Spelling and Vocabulary

Read the words below. Write the root words in the spaces provided.

1. irresponsible _____

2. misunderstand _____

3. meaningful _____

4. worthless _____

5. immaterial _____

6. disengage _____

7. unaware _____

8. prearrange _____

9. semicircle _____

10. biweekly _____

Put the following list of words in alphabetical order.

dandelion	quitter	underneath	hover
friend	other	violin	under
limb	cheese	xylophone	dandy
noise	season	yesterday	voice
otter	umbrella	salt	zebra

11. _____

12. _____

13. _____

14. _____

15. _____

16. _____

17. _____

18. _____

19. _____

20. _____

21. _____

22. _____

23. _____

24. _____

25. _____

26. _____

27. _____

28. _____

29. _____

30. _____

Capitalizing Proper Nouns

After reading the paragraph below, list eight proper nouns that should have been capitalized.

1. _____   5. _____

2. _____   6. _____

3. _____   7. _____

4. _____   8. _____

To the Farm

Last tuesday, which was the third of november, Lucille and her brother, Luke, left their home in the city of springfield. They traveled by train to a small town in indiana called richmond. When they arrived they were met by their grandparents, Lester and Lavonne Livingston, who live on a farm beside spoon river. After lunch Lucille and Luke helped their grandfather put some bales of hay into the back of the new pickup, a ford. Rover, the Livingstons' collie, hopped on top of the hay. Cuddles, the cat, tried to go along but ran away when Rover barked at her.

Find in the paragraph above 12 words used as common nouns. Write them on the lines below.

9. _____   15. _____

10. _____   16. _____

11. _____   17. _____

12. _____   18. _____

13. _____   19. _____

14. _____   20. _____

Capitalization for Proper Nouns and Direct Quotations

Put a **C** by those names which should be capitalized and an **N** by those which should remain lowercase.

1. _____ spain
2. _____ doctor johnson
3. _____ island
4. _____ prime minister blair
5. _____ maine
6. _____ lieutenant costa
7. _____ doctor
8. _____ louisiana
9. _____ captain
10. _____ january
11. _____ tuesday
12. _____ professor
13. _____ prime minister
14. _____ brooklyn bridge
15. _____ treaty of paris

16. _____ atlantic ocean
17. _____ lake
18. _____ colonel murphy
19. _____ professor hoover
20. _____ fourteenth amendment
21. _____ queen mary
22. _____ lieutenant
23. _____ yankee stadium
24. _____ month
25. _____ appalachians
26. _____ summer
27. _____ far west
28. _____ good friday
29. _____ southern
30. _____ manager

On the lines provided, capitalize correctly the following direct quotations.

31. lucille said, "we are not going to the Belvedere wedding after all."

_____

_____

32. "darling," said luke, "are you sure you do not want to go to the wedding?"

_____

_____

33. "after the way they behaved," said lucille, "it seems to me they do not deserve to have guests."

_____

_____

Capitalization for a Friendly Letter

Write a letter to a friend. You may choose someone who lives nearby or far away. Give special attention to the correct use of capital letters in the heading, salutation, and closing of your letter.

Assessment: Capitalization

Correct the capitalization in the following letter when you rewrite it below.

56565 highway b
monroe, louisiana 04321
september 1, 2003

dear lucille,

it has been a long time since i have seen you. just last night i was saying to rosa, "it has been a long time since i've seen lucy. someday soon we must go into town and see what she has been up to."

how are you doing in school? are you still making good grades? rosa and i are doing just fine. we like our teacher and are learning lots of new things.

the other day we saw captain jack. he is just fine. also, doctor beaulieau said to tell you "hello." let rosa and me know if you are going to be coming to monroe anytime soon.

sincerely yours,
Janelle

_____

_____

_____

_____

_____

_____

_____

_____

_____

_____

_____

_____

Using Periods and Question Marks

Use a period for a declarative sentence and a question mark for an interrogative sentence.
In each line there are two sentences. Write each sentence with the correct end punctuation.

1. My brother's name is Luke have you met him _____

   _____

2. The largest city in Texas is Houston have you been there _____

   _____

3. Your dog Penelope is very large does she bark loudly _____

   _____

4. I read the book called *The Call of the Wild* have you read it _____

   _____

5. Is that Ricardo sitting over there why is he laughing _____

   _____

6. What is the tallest building in town is it the city library _____

   _____

7. What is this green vegetable is it spinach _____

   _____

8. Why does a camel have a hump is it full of water _____

   _____

9. I have not seen Lucille for several days do you know where she is _____

   _____

10. Rosa said to me, "I have not seen Lucille for several days do you know where she is"

    _____

    _____

Using Quotation Marks

Quotation marks are used to indicate a speaker's or writer's exact words. Read the sentences and decide which ones need quotation marks.

☞ If a sentence is a direct quotation and needs quotation marks, write the sentence with the corrections.

☞ If the sentence is an indirect quotation, write it as a direct quotation.

Examples: Janelle said, I want to go now.   Janelle said, "I want to go now."

Janelle said she would stay here.   Janelle said, "I will stay here."

1. Ricardo said that he would be home in time for dinner. _____

_____

2. I told him that he should not stop at the video store on his way home. _____

_____

3. Ricardo said that he would not stop at the video store. _____

_____

4. I gently scolded Ricardo, You know what happens when you get into the video store.

_____

5. I reminded him that he was an hour late for dinner the last time. _____

_____

6. It won't happen this time, said Ricardo. I will be there and on time. _____

_____

7. I thought to myself, I'll believe it when I see him. _____

_____

8. I asked him if he would be bringing dinner home with him. _____

_____

9. He said that he thought we could eat the leftovers from the night before. _____

_____

10. Ricardo, I said, I ate the leftovers for lunch. _____

_____

11. He told me that he would surprise me with something for dinner. _____

_____

12. I told him I would look forward to his dinner surprise. _____

_____

Using Apostrophes

The apostrophe is used with nouns and indefinite pronouns to show possession. It is also used in contractions to indicate omitted words or letters.

> Examples: boy's cap; Luke's cap; men's cap; boys' caps; Jane's cap; Janes' caps; one's duty; others' duties; do not, don't; has not, hasn't; she is, she's; it is, it's

Find in each sentence the two words that require apostrophes and write them correctly on the lines.

1. Lukes father said that he couldnt go to my house after school today.

   _____   _____

2. All the Rosas names werent misspelled on the school roster.

   _____   _____

3. Therefore, my friend Rosas name wasnt spelled wrong.

   _____   _____

4. Shell make sure that your name isnt misspelled.

   _____   _____

5. After what Ive been through, itll be nice to have a chance to rest.

   _____   _____

6. My mothers seen to it that her daughters been very busy lately.

   _____   _____

7. Shes kept me working and has even made me do my brothers work.

   _____   _____

8. Thats one of the most unfair things Ive ever had to endure.

   _____   _____

9. I wouldve skipped his chores, but I couldnt get by with doing that.

   _____   _____

10. Its one of lifes most joyous moments when you realize all your work is done.

    _____   _____

11. Doing someone elses work shouldnt be part of my life.

    _____   _____

12. Im told that its not an unusual occurrence, no matter how old you are.

    _____   _____

Using Commas

☞ Commas are used with words in a series, with dates, and with names of cities and states.

Examples: Ricardo was tall, dark, and handsome. Ricardo was born June 30, 1993, in Odgen, Utah.

☞ Commas are used with greetings and closings in friendly letters.

Examples: Dear Ricardo,   Sincerely,

Insert commas where they belong in the following sentences when you rewrite them.

1. My best friends are Rosalie Lucille Ricardo and Lucas. _____
   _____

2. Rosalie was born in Ogden Utah on May 23 1994 at Ogden Hospital. _____
   _____

3. Her favorite pets are dogs cats goldfish and white mice._____
   _____

4. Lucille was born in Rochester New York on May 16 1994 at Rochester Hospital. _____
   _____

5. Lucille begins the letters she writes me with "Dear Louella" and then writes one two or ten pages._____
   _____

6. She wrote me that she visited Toronto Canada in June 2001 with her brother sister and parents._____
   _____

7. On January 1 2002 Ricardo wrote to tell me about his baseball football golf and hockey teams._____
   _____

8. He likes all kinds of sports and plays on every team his Austin Texas school has._____
   _____

9. He always signs his letters "Sincerely yours Ricardo" and sends them from Dallas Texas.
   _____

10. Lucas's letters end less formally with "See ya Lucas."_____
    _____

11. Always you can find Lucas playing tennis doubles with his friends Jules Julia and Jessamine. _____
    _____

12. It is always a treat to receive letters from Lucas Ricardo Rosalie and Lucille, all of whom were born in May 1994. _____
    _____

13. On January 10 2002 I sent letters to Ricardo Rosalie Lucas and Lucille._____
    _____

Assessment: Punctuation

Add commas, periods, apostrophes, and quotation marks where they are needed.

1. I havent celebrated Christmas with my fathers parents since I was two years old, I said.

   _____

   _____

2. They dont live near New York City New York anymore, and Im not able to see them often.

   _____

   _____

3. Yesterday I saw goldlfinches bluebirds scrub jays and sparrows at the feeder in our backyard. _____

   _____

4. Also yesterday I got a letter dated January 12 2002 from my friend in Tampa Florida.

   _____

   _____

5. Id like to visit Janice for Easter 2003 and also see my friends Esther Erica and Eileen.

   _____

   _____

6. Id never seen Dr A W Johnson without feeling ill until I saw him in L A. _____

   _____

7. L A stands for Los Angeles California, a very popular city in the U S. _____

   _____

8. Its just as well known in the U S as San Francisco California in the northern part of the state. _____

   _____

9. Are you sure thats true asked Daria I think that San Francisco may be better known.

   _____

   _____

10. Its very unusual for me to run into someone like Dr A W Johnson when Im in downtown LA. _____

    _____

Unit Assessment

Read the paragraph and answer the questions on this page and on page 42. Fill in the circles beside the correct answers.

My Favorite Transportation: A Book

1. When I want to visit some other part of the country or even the world, I dont need a plain
2. train or car. I cant call up a genie to grant my every wish, but I can find myself a good book to reed
3. Theres nothing like a book to take you anywhere you want to go while you expereince the comfort of
4. your own home. Where else could a person find such variety in her travels One book I read took me to
5. the grand canyon. It were an interesting way to see all aspects of the Canyon and its surroundings.
6. Another book carries me to new york city where I learn the history of the statue of Liberty. Recently me
7. had the oportunity to read a book that took me to the wide open spaces of the state of wyoming. I
8. had not never saw so many cattle and horses before. It is a real treet to travel this way.
9. Read a book and see the world.

---

line 1. How many words are misspelled?
- ⓐ one
- ⓑ two
- ⓒ three
- ⓓ four
- ⓔ none

How many apostrophe errors are there?
- ⓐ one
- ⓑ two
- ⓒ three
- ⓓ four
- ⓔ none

line 2. How many words are misspelled?
- ⓐ one
- ⓑ two
- ⓒ three
- ⓓ four
- ⓔ none

How many apostrophe errors are there?
- ⓐ one
- ⓑ two
- ⓒ three
- ⓓ four
- ⓔ none

line 3. How many words are misspelled?
- ⓐ one
- ⓑ two
- ⓒ three
- ⓓ four
- ⓔ none

How many apostrophe errors are there?
- ⓐ one
- ⓑ two
- ⓒ three
- ⓓ four
- ⓔ none

line 4. Which punctuation mark is missing?
- ⓐ comma
- ⓑ period
- ⓒ apostrophe
- ⓓ question mark
- ⓔ none

How many total errors are in line 4?
- ⓐ one
- ⓑ two
- ⓒ three
- ⓓ four
- ⓔ none

Unit Assessment *(cont.)*

line 5. How many words need to be capitalized?
    (a) one   (d) four
    (b) two   (e) none
    (c) three

Which word is misspelled?
    (a) interesting   (d) surroundings
    (b) aspects   (e) none
    (c) its

line 6. How many pronoun errors are there?
    (a) one   (d) four
    (b) two   (e) none
    (c) three

How many verb tense errors are there?
    (a) one   (d) four
    (b) two   (e) none
    (c) three

line 7. Which word is misspelled?
    (a) opportunity (d) state
    (b) read   (e) none
    (c) spaces

How many words need to be capitalized?
    (a) one   (d) four
    (b) two   (e) none
    (c) three

line 8. How many verb tense errors are there?
    (a) one   (d) four
    (b) two   (e) none
    (c) three

How many words are misspelled?
    (a) one   (d) four
    (b) two   (e) none
    (c) three

line 9. Which kind of sentence is it?
    (a) declarative (d) exclamatory
    (b) imperative (e) none of these
    (c) interrogative

Which is the subject of the sentence?
    (a) read   (d) you (understood)
    (b) book   (e) none of these
    (c) world

10. Which of these lines has a double negative?
    (a) line 1   (d) line 4
    (b) line 2   (e) none of these
    (c) line 3

11. Which of these lines has a wrong verb tense?
    (a) line 1   (d) line 3
    (b) line 2   (e) none of these
    (c) line 5

12. Which of these lines has no misspelled words?
    (a) line 1   (d) line 3
    (b) line 2   (e) none of these
    (c) line 4

13. Which line has four misspelled words?
    (a) lline 2   (d) line 8
    (b) line 4   (e) none of these
    (c) line 6

Unit Assessment *(cont.)*

Read the sentences and answer the questions.

1. Lucinda went to the store to by some new cloths.
2. Go to the store, Lucinda.
3. Did Lucinda go to the store as she was towed to do?
4. Why didn't Lucinda went to the store when she should've gone.
5. Go now!
6. Whenever I tells Lucinda to do something, she does this that or something else.
7. Me think that miss Lucinda is in for trouble the next time I see her.
8. Maybe Lucinda needs to spend less time with her freind Jocelyn or maybe she should have more work to do.
9. I think she should also spend less time watching television going to the movies and going to the maul.
10. It is time for me to have a talk with Lucinda and I think I will do that tomorrow.

---

1. Which sentence is imperative?
   - (a) 2
   - (b) 4
   - (c) 6
   - (d) 8
   - (e) none of these

2. Which sentence is interrogative?
   - (a) 2
   - (b) 4
   - (c) 6
   - (d) 8
   - (e) none of these

3. Which sentence is declarative?
   - (a) 2
   - (b) 3
   - (c) 4
   - (d) 5
   - (e) none of these

4. Which sentence is exclamatory?
   - (a) 1
   - (b) 4
   - (c) 5
   - (d) 7
   - (e) none of these

5. Which sentence contains the wrong pronoun?
   - (a) 5
   - (b) 7
   - (c) 8
   - (d) 9
   - (e) none of these

6. Which sentence contains a misspelled word?
   - (a) 2
   - (b) 3
   - (c) 5
   - (d) 7
   - (e) none of these

7. Which sentence uses the wrong verb form?
   - (a) 1
   - (b) 2
   - (c) 4
   - (d) 5
   - (e) none of these

8. Which of these sentences does not have any misspelled words?
   - (a) 2
   - (b) 3
   - (c) 8
   - (d) 9
   - (e) none of these

Unit Assessment *(cont.)*

Read these pairs of sentences and answer the questions below.

1. There is a City called Chicago and a City called Kansas City.
2. There is a city called Chicago and a city called Kansas City.

3. I know a tall boy named John.
4. I know a tall boy named John.

5. Next september Julie are going to live in Chicago.
6. Next September Julie are going to live in Chicago.

7. You can go to the movie, or you can go to the game.
8. You can go to the movie or you can go to the game.

9. Every Easter and Christmas we go on vacation to Los Angeles.
10. Every easter and christmas we go on vacation to Los Angeles.

---

1. Which sentence has no errors?
   - (a) 1
   - (b) 2
   - (c) both
   - (d) neither

2. Which sentence has capitalization errors?
   - (a) 5
   - (b) 6
   - (c) both
   - (d) neither

3. Which sentences contain no errors?
   - (a) 1, 2
   - (b) 3, 4
   - (c) 5, 6
   - (d) 7, 8

4. Which sentences do not have capitalization errors?
   - (a) 1, 2
   - (b) 3, 4
   - (c) 5, 6
   - (d) 9, 10

5. Which sentence has a capitalization error?
   - (a) 1
   - (b) 5
   - (c) both
   - (d) neither

6. Which sentence is missing a comma?
   - (a) 1
   - (b) 8
   - (c) both
   - (d) neither

7. Which sentences use the wrong verb form?
   - (a) 1, 2
   - (b) 9, 10
   - (c) both
   - (d) neither

8. Which sentence uses two holiday names correctly?
   - (a) 5
   - (b) 9
   - (c) both
   - (d) neither

Unit Assessment *(cont.)*

Choose the correct spelling.

1.
(a) experiense
(b) experence
(c) expereince
(d) experience

2.
(a) airplaine
(b) airplain
(c) airplane
(d) airplan

3.
(a) oportunity
(b) oprtunity
(c) oppurtunity
(d) opportunity

4.
(a) treet
(b) treat
(c) treit
(d) trete

5.
(a) puppy
(b) puppie
(c) pupy
(d) puppey

6.
(a) famiely
(b) faemily
(c) family
(d) famly

7.
(a) countrys
(b) cuntries
(c) cuntrys
(d) countries

8.
(a) February
(b) Febuary
(c) Februery
(d) Feberuary

9.
(a) ferniture
(b) furniture
(c) furnicher
(d) fernature

10.
(a) insex
(b) inseks
(c) insects
(d) insexts

11.
(a) giraffe
(b) geraffe
(c) gerrafe
(d) girrafe

12.
(a) vegatables
(b) vegatebles
(c) vegetables
(d) vejetables

13.
(a) lettuse
(b) lettuce
(c) leettus
(d) lettus

14.
(a) childern
(b) children
(c) childrun
(d) childsren

15.
(a) professer
(b) profeser
(c) proffesser
(d) professor

16.
(a) captian
(b) captain
(c) kaptin
(d) kaptain

17.
(a) screemed
(b) screimed
(c) screamed
(d) scriemed

18.
(a) different
(b) diffrent
(c) diefferent
(d) diffurent

19.
(a) mountins
(b) mowtins
(c) mountians
(d) mountains

20.
(a) sometimes
(b) sumtimes
(c) sommetimes
(d) sumetimes

21.
(a) roughley
(b) ruffley
(c) roughly
(d) ruffghley

Answer Key

Page 4
1. D
2. IT
3. E
4. IP
5. IT
6. D
7. D
8. E
9. E
10. D
11. D
12. D
13. E
14. D
15. IT

Page 6
Answers will vary. The following are sample responses.
1. Were you in Venice, Italy?
2. Oh, no!
3. Come with me to talk with Ms. Lee.
4. I plan to make all my grades above average by the end of the year.
5. Where is Scooter? Scooter, come here now. Scooter must be around here somewhere. Here comes Scooter!
6. Do I have to go? Let me go home right now. I don't want to go to Mars. No, I won't go!

Page 7
Answers for specific nouns will vary.
1. P, country
2. C, Monday
3. C, January
4. P, day
5. P, month
6. P, planet
7. P, city
8. P, country
9. P, holiday
10. C, Pacific Ocean
11. C, Mt. Washington
12. C, Belgium
13. P, state
14. P, mountain
15. P, lake
16. C, Easter
17. C, Los Angeles
18. C, Jamaica
19. C, Rover
20. C, Jumbo
21. P, car
22. C, Mrs. Lee
23. C, President Bush
24. C, Mayor Bradley
25. C, Earth
26. C, Kennedy Jr. High
27. P, lady/woman
28. P, apple/grandmother
29. C, "America"
30. C, "The Raven"

Page 8
1. ponies
2. chiefs
3. dances
4. zebras
5. radios
6. oranges
7. dresses
8. bushes
9. pianos
10. rodeos

Page 9
11. heroes
12. countries
13. enemies
14. fish
15. thieves
16. mice
17. women
18. deer
19. toothbrushes
20. Janes
21. Barneses
22. Marys

Page 10
1. He
2. it
3. She
4. They
5. They
6. her
7. it/him/her
8. He
9. him
10. it
11. It
12. them
13. She
14. her
15. She
16. him
17. We
18. they
19. It
20. They

Page 12
sample responses
1. caught
2. tapped
3. ran
4. bit
5. leave
6. run
7. Stop
8. lectured
9. bicycled
10. wrote

Page 13
1. played
2. were
3. was
4. broke
5. climbed
6. drew
7. understood
8. wrote
9. lost
10. tripped

Page 14
1. rang
2. rode
3. saw
4. ate
5. ran
6. will ring
7. will ride
8. will see
9. will eat
10. will run
paragraph
This <u>is</u> the year I <u>plan</u> improvements in my grades in school. Last year I <u>had</u> only average grades. My parents <u>said</u> they <u>thought</u> my grades <u>were</u> acceptable. I <u>was</u> glad they <u>felt</u> that way. However, I <u>think</u> that hard work <u>raises</u> a student's grades. Everyone <u>tells</u> me this <u>is</u> true, and I <u>believe</u> them. I now <u>plan</u> my days around school and homework. All other activities <u>come</u> after that. It <u>seems</u> to me that <u>is</u> the first step toward improvement. I <u>know</u> that if I <u>succeed</u> in school, the rewards <u>will come</u>. One reward <u>will be</u> more knowledge. Another reward <u>will be</u> good work habits. A further reward <u>will be</u> a chance for a better future.

Page 15
1. empty
2. open
3. fast
4. soft
5. raw
6. strong
7. green
8. black
9. blue
10. red
11. white
12. brown

Page 16
1. twelve
2. five
3. eight
4. seven
5. two
6. four
7.–15. Answers will vary. The following are sample responses.
7. These, those
8. This, that
9. These, those
10. Those, these
11 its
12. My
13. your
14. Her
15. their, our

Page 17
2. thin, thinner
3. lucky, luckiest
4. wiser, wisest
5. delicate, most delicate
6. green, greener

7. best
8. beautiful, more beautiful
9. stronger
10. most reliable
11. heavier
12. more delicious
13. bravest
14. hottest
15. redder
16. safest
17. colder
18. noisiest
19. luckier
20. biggest

Page 18
1. greedily
2. gently
3. silently
4. easily
5. slowly
6. noisily
11. strongly
12. sadly
13. neatly
14. slowly
15. carefully

Page 19
1. near
2. there/here
3. here/there
4. out
5. often
6. soon
7. now
8. yesterday
9. harder, hardest
10. softly, most softly
11. good, better
12. easier, easiest
13. fast, fastest

Page 20
sample responses
1. Jacqueline has a cat and a dog.
2. Would you rather have vanilla or chocolate ice cream?
3. I was going to play, but I decided to do homework.
4. Mother told me to come inside, but I stayed outside.
5. After school I have a swimming lesson and a piano lesson.
6. My favorite colors are blue and yellow.
7. I was going to ride my bike, but it had a flat tire.
8. We can have pizza or a hot dog for lunch.

Page 21
sample responses
1. You can wear your blue or black jeans.
2. Your white T-shirt fits better, but your red T-shirt is more colorful.
3. Do you want yellow or pink patches on your jeans?

Answer Key (cont.)

Page 21 (cont.)
4. Jillian's T-shirt looks attractive, and Jacqueline's jeans are stunning.
5. I have three pairs of blue jeans, but I want another pair.
6. You can wash your old jeans or iron your new jeans.
7. This white T-shirt is mine, and that white T-shirt is yours.
8. Let's wear our blue jeans today and our red jeans tomorrow.
9. My old jeans fit me well, but my new jeans do not.
10. I have washed my new red T-shirt but not my new blue T-shirt.

Page 22
1. I
2. C
3. C
4. I
5. I
6. C
7. I
8. I
9. I
10. I

Page 23
1. an
2. a
3. a
4. an
5. the
6. the
7. the
8. a
9. a
10. a
11. a
12. the
13. the
14. a
15. a
16. a
17. a
18. an
19. a/the
20. an/the
21. a/the
22. the
23. The
24. the
25. a/the

Page 24
1. on—a nest
2. into—its hole
3. under—the dining table
4. over—a fence
5. in—his very own house

6. before—the black horse
7. beside—her mother
8. toward—the fence
9. below—his high perch
10. inside—our house

Page 25
1.
Nouns
mother
cook
cake
year
prize
fair
flour
ingredients
bowl
egg
yolk
white
bowl
rest
ingredients
batter
pan
oven
minutes
cake
plate
knife
cake
Personal Pronouns
My
She
she
her
she
she
she
it
she
it
We
Verbs
is
prepared
won
added
cracked
dropped
mixed
put
was
put
cut
enjoyed
2.
Adjectives
My
an
outstanding
a
10-pound
rainbow
last
a
the
fishing
his
a

the
his
favorite
the
a
deep
the
the
perfect
his
the
a
half
a
soft
the
My
a
big
the
greatest
a
10-pound
rainbow
the
tournament
My
our
the
prizewinning
Adverbs
skillfully
easily
First
carefully
Then
expertly
next
Then
After
officially
Prepositional Phrases
at the fishing tournament
to the line
for his favorite spot
on the river
where the river curves
into the water
after a half hour
with the tournament committee

Page 26
sample sentences
1. Jack ran.
2. Little Jack ran.
3. Little Jack ran fast.
4. Little Jack quickly ran into the woods.
5. Into the woods Jack ran quickly.

Page 27
1. tale
2. hear
3. wood
4. pour
5. tail
6. here
7. poor
8. would

9. stare
10. towed
11. meet
12. mane
13. steel
14. weak
15. meddle
16. rode
17. mail
18. flour

Page 28
1. bark
2. bank
3. rock
4. bank
5. rock
6. bark
sample sentences
7. We dug a post hole.
8. He works in a post office.
9. He looks well.
10. He fell into the well.
11. The bat flew out of the cave.
12. He picked up the baseball bat.

Page 29
1. door
2. wash
3. agree
4. awake
5. finish
6. joy
7. bolt
8. phone
9. truth
10. claim
11. reason
12. respect
13. formal
14. prison
15. certain
16. suit
17. mistake
18. honor
19. break
20. construct

Page 30
1. fish
2. pan
3. corn
4. mother
5. brush
6. quake
7. ache
8. coat
9. prints
10. where
11. strawberry
12. moonlight
13. photograph
14. breakfast
15. lifeboat
16. handcuffs
17. football
18. notebook

Page 31
1. response

2. understand
3. meaning
4. worth
5. material
6. engage
7. aware
8. arrange
9. circle
10. week
11. cheese
12. dandelion
13. dandy
14. friend
15. hover
16. limb
17. noise
18. other
19. otter
20. quitter
21. salt
22. season
23. umbrella
24. under
25. underneath
26. violin
27. voice
28. xylophone
29. yesterday
30. zebra

Page 32
1. Tuesday
2. November
3. Springfield
4. Indiana
5. Richmond
6. Spoon
7. River
8. Ford
(18 possible answers)
third
brother
home
city
train
town
grandparents
farm
lunch
grandfather
bales
hay
back
pickup
collie
top
hay
cat

Page 33
1. C
2. C
3. N
4. C
5. C
6. C
7. N
8. C
9. N
10. C
11. C
12. N
13. N
14. C

Answer Key (cont.)

Page 33 (cont.)
15. C
16. C
17. N
18. C
19. C
20. C
21. C
22. C
23. C
24. N
25. C
26. N
27. C
28. C
29. N
30. N
31. Lucille said, "We are not going to the Belvedere wedding after all."
32. "Darling," said Luke, "are you sure you do not want to go to the wedding?"
33. "After the way they behaved," said Lucille, "it seems to me they do not deserve to have guests."

Page 34
sample heading, salutation, closing
6654 Highway C
Amos, Iowa 01234
January 1, 2003

Dear Sally,
Sincerely yours,

Page 35
56565 Highway B
Monroe, Louisiana 04321
September 1, 2003
Dear Lucille,
It has been a long time since I have seen you. Just last night I was saying to Rosa, "It has been a long time since I've seen Lucy. Someday soon we must go into town and see what she has been up to."
How are you doing in school? Are you still making good grades? Rosa and I are doing just fine. We like our teacher and are learning lots of new things.
The other day we saw Captain Jack. He is just fine. Also, Doctor Beaulieu said to tell you "Hello." Let Rosa and me know if you are going to be coming to Monroe anytime soon.
Sincerely yours,
Janelle

Page 36
1. My brother's name is Luke. Have you met him?
2. The largest city in Texas is Houston. Have you been there?
3. Your dog Penelope is very large. Does she bark loudly?
4. I read the book called *The Call of the Wild*. Have you read it?
5. Is that Ricardo sitting over there? Why is he laughing?
6. What is the tallest building in town? Is it the city library?
7. What is the green vegetable? Is it spinach?
8. Why does a camel have a hump? Is it full of water?
9. I have not seen Lucille for several days. Do you know where she is?
10. Rosa said to me, "I have not seen Lucille for several days. Do you know where she is?"

Page 37
sample responses
1. Ricardo said, "I will be home in time for dinner."
2. I told him, "You should not stop at the video store on your way home."
3. Ricardo said, "I will not stop at the video store."
4. I gently scolded Ricardo, "You know what happens when you get into the video store."
5. I reminded him, "You were an hour late for dinner the last time."
6. "It won't happen this time," said Ricardo. "I will be there and on time."
7. I thought to myself, "I'll believe it when I see him."
8. I asked him, "Will you be bringing dinner home with you?"
9. He said, "I thought we could eat the leftovers from last night."
10. "Ricardo," I said, "I ate the leftovers for lunch."
11. He told me, "I will surprise you with something for dinner."
12. I told him, "I will look forward to your dinner surprise."

Page 38
1. Luke's, couldn't
2. Rosas', weren't
3. Rosa's, wasn't
4. She'll, isn't
5. I've, it'll
6. mother's, daughter's
7. She's, brother's
8. That's, I've
9. would've, couldn't
10. It's, life's
11. else's, shouldn't
12. I'm, it's

Page 39
1. My best friends are Rosalie, Lucille, Ricardo, and Lucas.
2. Rosalie was born in Odgen, Utah, on May 23, 1994, at Ogden Hospital.
3. Her favorite pets are dogs, cats, goldfish, and white mice.
4. Lucille was born in Rochester, New York, on May 16, 1994, at Rochester Hospital.
5. Lucille begins the letters she writes me with "Dear Louella," and then writes one, two, or ten pages.
6. She wrote me that she visited Toronto, Canada, in June 2001 with her brother, sister, and parents.
7. On January 1, 2002, Ricardo wrote to tell me about his baseball, football, golf, and hockey teams.
8. He likes all kinds of sports and plays on every team his Austin, Texas, school has.
9. He always signs his letters, "Sincerely yours, Ricardo" and sends them from Dallas, Texas.
10. Lucas's letters end less formally with "See ya, Lucas"
11. Always you can find Lucas playing doubles tennis with his friends Jules, Julia, and Jessamine.
12. It is always a treat to receive letters from Lucas, Ricardo, Rosalie, and Lucille, all of whom were born in May 1994.
13. On January 10, 2002, I sent letters to Ricardo, Rosalie, Lucas, and Lucille.

Page 40
1. "I haven't celebrated Christmas with my father's parents since I was two years old," I said.
2. They don't live near New York City, New York, anymore, and I'm not able to see them often.
3. Yesterday I saw goldfinches, bluebirds, scrub jays, and sparrows at the feeder in our backyard.
4. Also yesterday I got a letter dated January 12, 2002, from my friend in Tampa, Florida.
5. I'd like to visit Janice for Easter 2003 and also see my friends Esther, Erica, and Eileen.
6. I'd never seen Dr. A.W. Johnson without feeling ill until I saw him in L.A.
7. L.A. stands for Los Angeles, California, a very popular city in the U.S.
8. It's just as well known in the U.S. as San Francisco, California, in the northern part of the state.
9. "Are you sure that's true?" asked Daria. "I think that San Francisco may be better known."
10. It's very unusual for me to run into someone like Dr. A. W. Johnson when I'm in downtown L.A.

Pages 41–42
line 1. a., a.
line 2. a., a.
line 3. b., a.
line 4. d., a.
line 5. b., e.
line 6. a., b.
line 7. a., a.
line 8. a., a.
line 9. b., d.
10. e
11. c
12. c
13. e

Page 43
1. a
2. b
3. e
4. c
5. b
6. b
7. c
8. a

Page 44
1. b
2. a
3. b
4. b
5. c
6. b
7. d
8. b

Page 45
1. d
2. c
3. d
4. b
5. a
6. c
7. d
8. a
9. b
10. c
11. a
12. c
13. b
14. b
15. d
16. b
17. c
18. a
19. d
20. a
21. c